W9-CDU-602

THE TIDE OF NATIONALISM

also by Abba Eban

VOICE OF ISRAEL

ABBA EBAN

THE TIDE OF NATIONALISM

HORIZON PRESS NEW YORK 1959

The Tide of Nationalism
The Third Herbert Samuel Lecture

Library of Congress Catalog Card Number 59-12813
Manufactured in the United States of America

Map of the Middle East and the Mediterranean

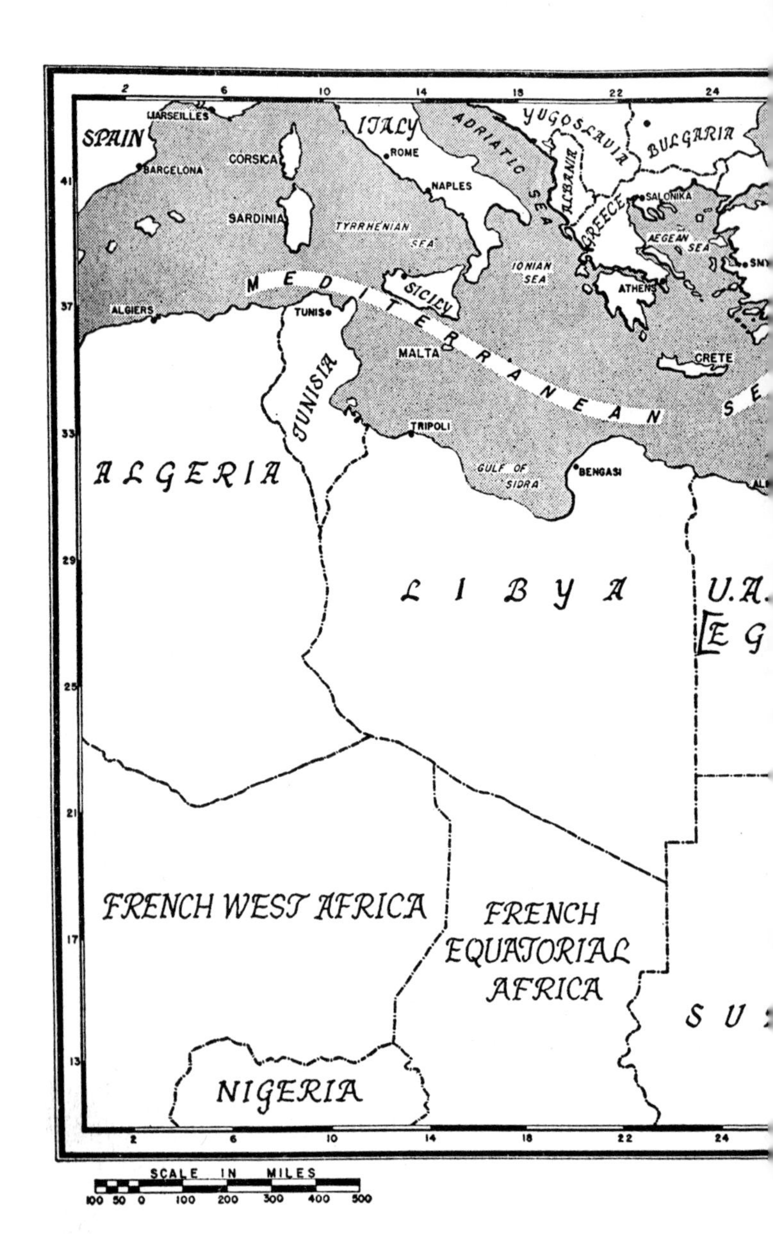
SPAIN
MARSEILLES
BARCELONA
CORSICA
SARDINIA
ALGIERS
ITALY
ROME
NAPLES
TYRRHENIAN SEA
ADRIATIC SEA
YUGOSLAVIA
ALBANIA
BULGARIA
GREECE
SALONIKA
AEGEAN SEA
ATHENS
IONIAN SEA
SICILY
MEDITERRANEAN SE
TUNIS
TUNISIA
MALTA
CRETE
TRIPOLI
GULF OF SIDRA
BENGASI
ALGERIA
LIBYA
U.A.
[EG
FRENCH WEST AFRICA
FRENCH EQUATORIAL AFRICA
SU
NIGERIA
SCALE IN MILES
100 50 0 100 200 300 400 500

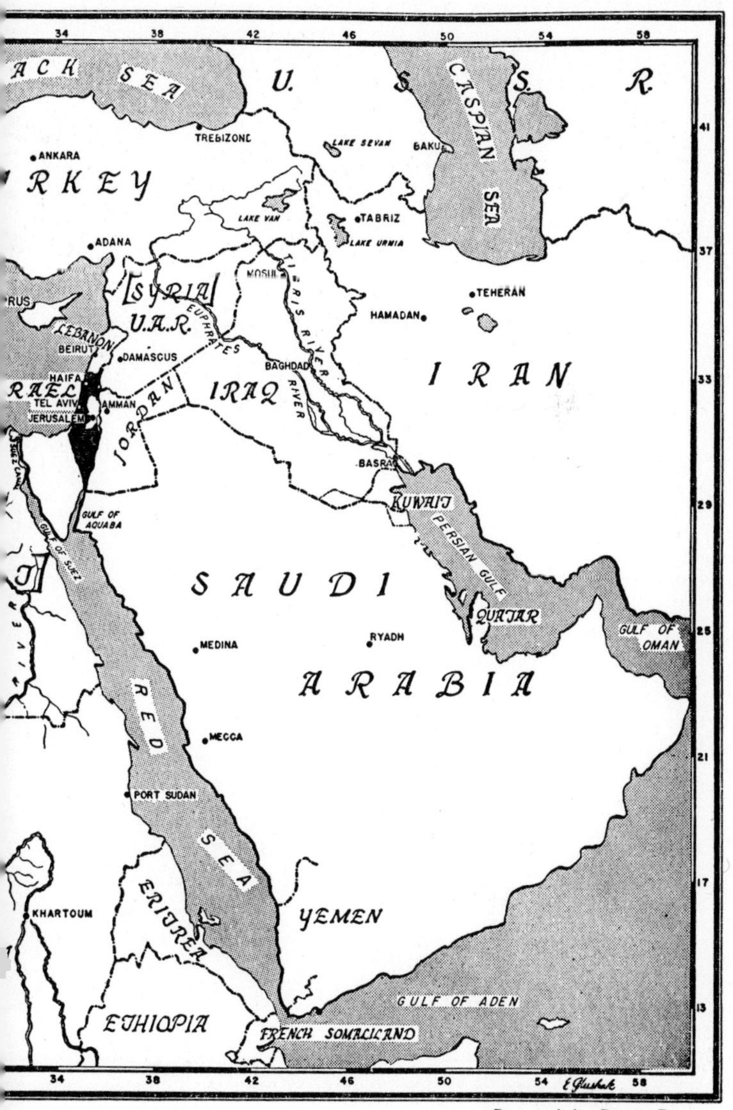

By permission Beacon Press

I

In delivering the third Herbert Samuel lecture I tread in honored footsteps; first in those of Gilbert Murray, the ornament of Oxford life and the brilliant interpreter of Hellenic civilization to many generations; and second, in those of Sir Isaiah Berlin, who last year shed a true and gracious light on the work and character of the incomparable Chaim Weizmann.

This series of lectures bears a name which I have held in reverence since my early youth. Perhaps I may evoke an association of memory. Twenty-two years ago it was my duty to confront Lord Samuel in a debate in the Cambridge Union. I presume that the tradition of these gladiatorial contests still endures. A great lion from the world of politics or learning, secure in the eminence of his fame, is brought down to speak; and an undergraduate is thrown into the arena to be decorously devoured. Lord Samuel was the lion, and I was the victim. I felt very much like Daniel in the lions' den—except that our renowned ancestor was not alone; and he could rely in his ordeal on Divine salvation, which I invoked vainly in my cause. The years have rolled on, and I have enjoyed many reunions with our eminent Chairman of which the most moving is that which takes place tonight.

Lord Samuel is the nearest approach in the modern history of nations to Plato's ideal of the philosopher statesman. Plato laid down rigid standards of scholarship and integrity as the qualification for political leadership. If these standards were rigorously applied today, many governments, alas, might become seriously depleted.

Learning as a quality of statesmanship is also

a Hebrew ideal. Ancient Israel, both in the First and Second Commonwealths, respected the political counsel of literate men whose minds revolved within a broad view of national and universal destiny. Today, in its new era of independence, Israel may enlarge her stature beyond the limits of her territory and population in the measure that she gives expression to her potentialities of mind and spirit. This prospect, however, depends on her ability to bring the most vital intellectual forces of the nation into contact with the concerns and responsibilities of government.

II

Our theme this evening is the tide of nationalism. It is the most potent influence in the life of our times. The golden age of nationalism in Europe and America was the period between the end of the eighteenth and the end of the nineteenth century. The greatest milestones in the advance were the American and French Revolutions. As the nineteenth century went on its course, the main contours of the world's national groups became fixed in their contemporary pattern. The major powers, with the exception of the Ottoman and Austro-Hungarian Empires, corresponded in their political structure to some identifiable form of cultural and ethnic unity. The struggles of emergent nationalisms were sustained by liberal sympathies. The word was associated with the efforts of small peoples to rid themselves of foreign domination. It was surrounded by an air of chivalry and grace. But as the years advanced and the greater nations became secure in their political freedom, the word "nationalism" fell on evil days. By a typical psychic attitude nations which had consolidated their liberty looked condescendingly on the struggles of those who had not yet reached the shore. The leaders of European nations regarded those who had not yet attained their freedom with something of the distaste felt by those who have just dined towards the spectacle of a well-stocked table. The word "narrow" became the conventional epithet of nationalism. It was always the nationalism of other nations that was narrow. The concept was associated with its own excesses. First the face of nationalism was painted "with its warts;" and then the original face disappeared entirely and only the blemishes remained. This optical maneuver still persists in many places. There is a quality of devotion to people and country which men call "patriotism" when they possess it themselves, and "chauvinism" when they observe it in others. The discredit of nationalism was achieved by contrasting it with the broad universality which would prevail if only other peoples' nationalism would become less obsessive, more enlightened, in a word, less "narrow."

In our own day the pendulum has swung back. Nationalism is again a favored word and no longer held to be incompatible with a broad universality. Internationalism and nationalism are not conceived as antithetical terms. Internationalism, after all, is nothing but a Latin word signifying a relationship between nations; and the individual nation-state is still the only recognized unit of the international society. Variations of culture and language, of artistic and literary expression, which are the essence of national distinctiveness, are rightly seen as part of the creative diversity of our world. The political outlook and social organization of a people are as integral a part of its culture as are its language, art and music. All these variations, of culture and of political ideas, are part of the world's mental and spiritual landscape, just as mountains, valleys and oceans are part of its diverse physical fabric. To cry out for uniformity, to dream of a monolithic world government which would obliterate the character of nations, is no more intelligent than to long for an earth which would lose its physical differences, its contours and heights, the divisions of its lands and waters.

The United Nations Charter which governs the legal relationships between States is strongly anchored in the doctrine of national sovereignty, subject to restraints and sanctions voluntarily accepted in the interests of the world community.

Just as individual citizenship with its private rights is limited by national duty, so are the rights of nations qualified, though not impaired, by the system of international obligations set forth in the Charter. This document strikes a magnificent balance between the dignity and freedom of nations and the broader interests of a universal society.

III

But the center of gravity has shifted in the nationalist discussion of today. The debate is no longer about Europe. Its themes are set in Asia and Africa. A great pageant of emancipation has unfolded in those two continents. It is difficult not to be astonished by the speed and scope of the transformation. These continents, which only a few decades ago lay under foreign yoke, are now a lively scene of national independence. The progress is reflected in the statistics of international life. The United Nations has grown in membership from 52 to 82 within the past decade. Nor is the progress yet finished. By 1960 six new independent African sovereignties will have joined us, including Nigeria, Somaliland, the Togolands and the Cameroons. And this comes after the rich harvest of national freedom garnered in Asia during the past two decades. Professor Toynbee, about whose infallibility I hold certain heretical reservations, has stated that the day of the nation-state is over, and that the future belongs to supra-national agglomerations such as the old Millet system of the Ottoman Empire. If the nation-state is in decline, it is certainly a most fruitful and vigorous collapse. Scarcely a year passes without some enrichment of the international tapestry through the addition of a nation representing a new shade in culture and civilization.

Nothing in this process of liberation has been more spectacular than the advance of the Arab nation towards its freedom. The Arab people has achieved its independence in ten sovereign States, covering four million square miles and a population of 70 million. This vast expanse is rich in natural and mineral wealth. It comprises all the centers of civilization in which the Arab mind reached its highest radiance—Cairo and Damascus, Baghdad and the Holy Cities of the Arabian Peninsula. Never in history has the Arab nation commanded such lavish political and economic opportunities as those which now lie in its grasp. The opportunities of today are enriched by the memories of yesterday. A long historic tradition and a proud cultural legacy are amongst the assets which Arab nationalism carries with it into its future. Within a few decades the Arab nation has traversed the chasm from total subjection to an almost complete emancipation.

It might therefore have been expected that Arab nationalism would face the world in a demeanor of victory, not of savage grievance. But the liberated Arab peoples still live in a psychic world marked by three circles of tension: first, in their relations with each other; second, in their relations with the Western world; and third, in their relations with Israel. The primary error of Western minds in the contemplation of Arab nationalism has been to overestimate the third of these circles of tension—that with Israel—and to underestimate the other two—the problem of inter-Arab relations, and the tension between the Arab world and the West.

It is not for others to determine the ultimate relationship between the independent Arab nations. Scholars have long seen two tendencies at work in the Middle East: the one making for centralization and union, the other emphasizing regional differences, decentralization, diversity, separatism. The pull between these two forces has determined a great part of Middle Eastern history, and I doubt if it will soon be resolved by any clear-cut formula.

There is certainly no truth in the historic fatalism which holds that union is the only natural condition of Arab history, and that any assertion of separatism within the Arab family is an offense against historic compulsions. Union has not been the general condition of Arab history. Indeed, except for two brief periods, once under the early Caliphate and once under Saladin, the various parts of the Arab world have always refused to come under a centralized domination. Union has been the exception, not the rule. In particular, a separation of Arab life between two main centers, one in the Nile Valley and the other in the Euphrates, has been a constant tradition. I doubt if it will be broken now by establishing the hegemony of the Nile Valley over the Fertile Crescent.

During the exceptional periods of centralized control, the union of the Arab world was achieved not by voluntary submission but by military coercion. Whenever the strongest military power in the Arab world was unable to impose its domination upon the whole expanse, fragmentation set in, acts of secession took place and the geographical and cultural diversities of the Arab subcontinent asserted themselves. It has been more normal in history for various parts of the Arab world to be apart than for them to be together. And this separatist, particularist tendency existed fully during the eras of Arab independence. It is not the artificial result of disruptive policies practiced by the Great Powers in the past century.

IV

The greatest single factor of Arab unity has been that of language and culture. The Arab mind has always been dominated by a deep pride of heritage. Its contours are formed, its spirit expressed in a language of rich and potent variety. There is an Arabic literature of such versatility and range as to constitute a full humanistic education in itself. Apart from its contributions to the humane arts and to philosophy, the Arab mind has achieved radiant insight into the natural sciences; and of all this diverse and copious tradition the Arabic language is the indispensable master-key.

But this cultural unity is not unreserved. It is limited by variations of dialect and, still more, by the cultural apathy of those who have not achieved a basic literacy. Owing to the backward state of public education, the enrichment of this cultural legacy lies beyond the general access of Arab peoples. Nevertheless this cultural unity exists, and the sentimental impulses which it evokes cannot be underestimated. There is a way of speaking and thinking, of rejoicing and suffering, of loving and, above all, I fear, of hating, which is typically and uniquely Arab. It is to this unifying ethos that Arab politicians appeal when they seek to decry the separate nationhood of Arab States in favor of the Nasserist concept of one People, one State—and, of course, one Leader.

V

But cultural affinity, however profound, does not settle the issue of political unity. Unity of language is not in itself a justification for the domination of one State by another. Few living memories are too short to recall the part which the concept of linguistic unity played in the early phase of Nazi expansion in Europe. It was deemed to be the right of the German Reich to bring under its single domination all those who were of Germanic tongue. Linguistic unity became a springboard for a movement aiming to destroy the separate identity and personality of States.

In the opposite sense, the relationship between linguistic unity and political separatism can be vividly illustrated from the example of Latin

America. There we see eighteen States bound by a linguistic and cultural unity at least as strong as that prevailing between the Arab States. But each Latin Republic conserves its political identity and its juridical personality without challenge or grudge. No man of liberal mind has ever suggested that in the name of linguistic affinity the strongest Latin republic has a "right" to dominate its weaker neighbors. Political separatism and cultural unity are completely reconcilable. The relations across the parallel between the United States and Canada are another example of this. There is a strong community of language and culture and, at the same time, a clear separation of political tradition and outlook. Perhaps the same could be said of the relationships between the United Kingdom and the United States of America—two kindred but separate nations whose languages, when written, bear a striking resemblance to each other.

Let it therefore not be believed that community of language creates a historic determinism in favor of a unified Arab land mass, destroying the present frontiers of States.

The same conclusion is reached if we look at the juridical history of Arab nationalism. Arab liberation has taken place in the context of separate nationhoods. This fact of history cannot be denied its impact on future events. The United Nations has been the main arena in which the evolution of Arab freedom has been played out. This gives crucial importance to the law of the Charter as a factor governing the forms and moods of Arab nationalism. The Arab States are organized internationally as ten distinct sovereignties within the United Nations.

The multiple representation of Arab nations means that the relations of these ten States with each other are governed by the rights and obligations, the disciplines and restraints, which prevail between all members of the United Nations' family. The Charter does not obstruct voluntary union between States, but it does protect the right of any State to maintain its separate identity, should it so desire. It stands at the crossroads dividing voluntary union from coercion.

It is often said that the world "must come to terms with Arab nationalism." Surely there is a prior condition—that Arab nationalism must come to terms with the Charter, and with the rights of other nations. If the slogan about "coming to terms with nationalism" means that we must respect the right of each Arab nation to live in sovereignty and peace, then we must certainly come to terms with this ambition, not only for Arab States but for other States as well. But if "coming to terms" with Arab nationalism means that we must condone the right of one Arab nation to extend its hegemony and domination over others, and that those who resist such domination must be assailed by infiltration, by subversion, by incitement and by threat of assassination, then we can come to terms with such a nationalism on one condition alone—that we take the Charter of the United Nations and tear it into small pieces and throw the pieces upon the fire. The fact that the Arab people are represented by ten separate sovereignties gives the other 72 members of the international community a right, indeed a duty, to control the relations between the ten, when these affect international peace and security. This fact was recognized last year by the action of Arab governments, such as those of Lebanon, Jordan and Sudan, which brought complaints against the United Arab Republic to international tribunals. By submitting such complaints to a non-Arab forum they recognized that inter-Arab relations are not purely of internal or family concern. If the Arab land mass were under one sovereignty, with a single international personality, the relations between its separate provinces would be of domestic and not international interest. Since this multiple representation of Arab nationalism is one of the sources of its political strength, the limitations and restraints of the system must also be accepted.

VI

I have spoken of factors of history, politics and law which create strong separatist impulses in the Arab world, side by side with the admittedly strong pull of unity. The economic factor reinforces this separation. The economies of the Arab States are not complementary or even similar except in some of their weaknesses. The tension between the oil States—Iraq, the Arabian Peninsula and the Persian Gulf—and the States which lack this source of revenue is crucial. Nothing has happened in recent months to bring about a redistribution of these revenues across the frontiers of Arab States. The economic policies of most Arab States are concerned with the resources within their separate frontiers and with bilateral relations reaching far beyond the Middle East.

There is less inter-State economic cooperation in the Arab world than in Western Europe.

The conflict between the regional and the unilateral approach to economic development has been illustrated very recently. In August 1958 the President of the United States offered economic assistance to Arab states, conditioned by their willingness to cooperate in economic and social development. There was no response to this offer. Inter-Arab relationships were not sufficiently cooperative to bring a collective agency into being. Later the Government of the United Arab Republic was offered economic aid for the Aswan Dam by the Soviet Union on a strictly unilateral basis, not even involving the other riparian States of the Nile. The first offer, based on Arab cooperation, was not accepted. The second was exultantly received.

VII

Against the factors of history, politics, law and economics which have given a separate nationhood to Arab peoples, there has arisen Nasser's concept of nationalism described in his book *The Philosophy of a Revolution.* Many of Nasser's troubles come from his attempt to be the hero of his own book. Nasserism is not necessarily committed to an Arab union which would merge Arab sovereignties into a single statehood. This complete form of union has been tried in one area. Syria has achieved the kind of "union" with Egypt which our ancestor Jonah achieved with the whale—and the gastric rumblings from Damascus and Cairo show that the digestion has been neither smooth nor effective. But even if he finds this form of union to be too integral for future emulation, the fact remains that Nasser does not accept the concept of equality between Arab States. His is a doctrine of nationalism based on one main point of gravity. A truly Arab government in the vocabulary of Nasserism is one which acknowledges Cairo's suzerainty. All others are "agents of imperialism." Arab governments which have chosen to have close relations with the West, such as those of Bourguiba in Tunis, Chamoun in Lebanon or Khalil in Sudan, are "treacherous" to nationalism. Subservience to a non-Western power, provided that it is practiced by Nasser himself, is "independence." Cairo is to be the sole center for determining the policies of the Arab governments in their international relationships. This concept of Nasser's rightful hegemony has made fantastic headway amongst intellectual and political activists in the Arab countries. It is less easy to understand its attraction for men of liberal mind in the Western world.

Sometimes the claim of Nasserism to dominate other Arab governments is supported on the grounds that his victims are reactionary. From the international viewpoint this is an irrational criterion. Under the law of the Charter "reactionary" and "non-reactionary governments" have an equal right to be protected against aggressive assault. In any normal society a citizen's right to protection does not depend upon the "progressive" nature of his convictions. In 1939 the free world went to war in support of Poland. Enough time has passed to establish a Statute of Limitations under which even a working diplomat may now cast doubt upon the progressive radiance of the Beck regime in the Poland of 1939. But the right of that country to be protected by collective security was intrinsic and could not be gainsaid. The doctrine that

Middle Eastern Governments should be abandoned to Nasserist control because they have not reached perfection in progressiveness must be rejected. An even more pertinent question is whether Nasserism can seriously sustain its claim to be more progressive than the regimes which it seeks to dominate or subvert. Is there any police state more rigid, any despotism more acute, than that which prevails under the Nasserist system? The Lebanon of Chamoun and Shehab has its evident imperfections. But it holds the seed of a constitutional principle which once flourished in Cairo and has now been smothered. Nasserism with its rigged elections and its single party system cannot claim to satisfy the standards of Jeffersonian democracy. Similarly, the Arab Governments of Africa, and even of Iraq under both its recent regimes, have shown a more constructive instinct for economic advancement than the allegedly "progressive" leader of the Arab continent has displayed in his own country. Therefore even if it could be admitted that a superior level of "progressiveness" was a title to domination, those credentials would not belong to Nasser in relation to any of his neighbors.

The concept of "Arab unity" as espoused by the Nasserist movement therefore needs critical scrutiny. It cannot be endorsed in fatalistic resignation. A system of separate States, free to determine their cooperation with Cairo, with each other and with all others is essentially more progressive than that which speaks of an "irresistible tide" of Nasserism to which all who respect nationalism must yield. A few decades ago an attempt was made to unify Europe by subversion and force. That movement for continental unity left behind a fearful toll of agony and havoc. Today the peoples of Western Europe are building their community in freedom and consent, with no renunciation of their identity as sovereign States. A selective judgment would surely endorse the second and reject the first of these concepts of continental unity. This is a matter in which the means are no less decisive than the ends.

A normal Arab nationalism is therefore not necessarily one that finds expression in a vast agglomeration of territory with one single center of effective control. It can better be reflected in a constellation of kindred States each with its separate authority and identity.

VIII

Nothing has divided the Arab world more fiercely than the attempt to unify it. At one time it seemed as if the Pan-Arab sentiment proclaimed from Cairo with its imposing apparatus of radio and press propaganda would sweep all dissentient Arab opinion aside. Syria became an Egyptian province, Lebanon and Jordan were of dubious stability or viability. The Iraqi revolution appeared to augur Nasserist control.

But since the latter half of 1958 the particularist tendencies in Arab nationalism have asserted themselves with impressive strength. It seems as if there is nothing that an Arab nation will not do to save itself from the unwanted embrace of Cairo's jurisdiction. Even the acceptance of foreign military aid is deemed preferable to a fatalistic acceptance of Egyptian control. Lebanon has called for American troops, Jordan for British forces at the height of their desperate defense of their integrity. Iraq, in the torment of Nasserist pressure, has involved herself in a closer relationship with the Soviet Union than she would have done without Nasserist subversion threatening the independence of her regime. In each case the Great Power involvement has been a secondary result—a reaction to an unendurable tension within Arab nationalism itself. Nasserism which proclaimed its ambition of saving Arab nations from the interventions of Great Power influences has, in fact, brought about a more constant embroilment of the Great Powers in the Arab world than any other movement ever wished or managed to do. In his denunciation of Communist influence in the Middle East, Nasser is very much like a man who sets fire to a house and then complains of the heat of the blaze.

There are some inside and outside the Middle East who doubt the accuracy of ascribing these constant tensions to the pressure of Nasserism. The skeptics and apologists, however, have never been able to explain the astonishing volume of complaint and apprehension which Nasserist policies have evoked in the region. Iraq, Jordan, Lebanon, Tunis and Sudan have all, at various times in the past two years, raised cries of alarm and indignation at Nasserist encroachment on their independence. In Turkey, Iran and Ethiopia it is both held and widely proclaimed that an expansionist force, disrespectful of the existing structure of sovereignties, is rampant in the Middle East. Newly emergent African nations have a similar irritation. If all these are wrong in their complaints and fears, then Nasserism has evoked an inexplicable and remarkably versatile apprehension.

IX

But the relations of Arab States with each other are only one part of the Middle Eastern tension. There is also the problem of Arab relations with the West. The crisis in this relationship has profound historic roots. In its outlook upon the West and upon itself the Arab mind has passed through three sharp phases. In the first of these it enjoyed a feeling of superiority. Light and learning reposed in the East, while the West lay beyond the pale of culture. I will illustrate this by recalling what a tenth century Arab geographer, Al Masudi, had to say about Europe:

> "The peoples of the north are those for whom the sun is distant from the zenith. . . . Cold and damp prevail in those regions,

> and snow and ice follow one another in endless succession. The warm humor is lacking amongst them: their bodies are large, their natures gross, their manners harsh, their understanding dull and their tongues heavy. Their religious beliefs lack solidity. Those of them who are farthest to the north are the most subject to grossness and brutishness."

Nothing could be clearer than that. From this sense of aristocratic superiority, fully justified by the radiance of Arab achievement in that epoch, the Arabs passed into a phase of subjection to European rule and a reluctant acknowledgement of Europe's superiority. This phase lasted until the end of the First World War which heralded the first progress in Arab political emancipation. Today, we are in the third phase. The Arab people can no longer look upon the West in the contemptuous terms of the tenth century geographer; and it cannot seriously claim that it is dominated or humiliated by the West. But the Nasserists refuse to believe the second of these facts. They decline to admit that Western domination has gone away. They pursue their "imperialist" adversary far beyond the point of his own retreat. They pass from a defense of their own outraged rights to a violation of the rights of others. The seizure of Suez and the anti-Israel boycott are evidence of this. It is not enough for Arab nationalists to achieve equality by avoiding injury to their own interests or pride. There is a perverse insistence on settling accounts. The injuries once inflicted by the West on the pride and interests of the Arab nations must now be returned in kind.

Let us not underestimate the depth of this tension. Arab hostility to the West is not organically linked with the problem of Arab-Israel relationships. Indeed, Arab antagonism to the West antedates, transcends and may well survive Arab hostility to Israel. The roots of the tension between the Arab and the Western worlds are far deeper than the more superficial and limited Arab-Israel conflict. It is instructive to find the West embroiled in crisis with Asian and African nationalism in areas where the Israel issue has no real echo—all the way from Indonesia to Algeria, from Afghanistan to Morocco. This itself should bring into question the belief of some experts on the Middle East that the relations of the West with Arab nationalism would be idyllic or even tranquil "but for Israel." Quite apart from the Israel issue, the major Western Powers have not succeeded in finding a new level of mutual trust on which to meet the emergent nationalisms of today in their curiously mixed mood of triumph and suspicion.

X

Beyond the relations of the Arab States with each other and with the West lies the neglected problem of the non-Arab Middle East. Together with the liberation of the Arab peoples, other nations in the Middle East have secured their liberties. One people—Israel—older than any in the continuity of its language, tradition and sense of peoplehood, has been restored to its independence, albeit within a domain more modest than that in which Arab national freedom has been achieved. The existence and progress of Turkey, of Iran, of Ethiopia, serve to remind us that other important parts of the Middle East lie outside the range of Arab nationhood. The sovereignties of Africa include nations which are an organic part of the Middle

Eastern expanse. It is vital, therefore, to recall that the Middle East and the Arab world are not equivalent or identical terms.

The Middle East, as defined in the general practice of the United Nations, is inhabited by some 60 million Arabs, taking language as the broadest criterion, and by 75 million non-Arabs. There is a non-Arab Middle East extending from Turkey and Persia through Israel to Ethiopia; and if we extend the area to include Afghanistan and Pakistan, then the predominantly non-Arab character of the region becomes even more manifest. It follows that official Arab declarations about a continuous area extending between the Atlantic Ocean and the Persian Gulf as the inheritance of any one nation must be regarded as an offense against international peace as well as a distortion of history, geography and law. While full respect is due to the rights of Arab nations, it remains true that the

Middle East has not been in the past, is not now and can never be in the future an exclusively Arab domain.

The inner, progressive truth about the Middle East is to be found not in the word "unity" but in the greater words "diversity" and "tolerance." Our region has known its real glories only when these were its themes. There is not one Arab nationalism alone. There are several Arab nations united by the United Nations Charter with each other and with all others, and showing a rich variety of regional and cultural divergencies. There is not only Islam. The older Middle Eastern faiths have their authentic abodes in the Middle East—Judaism as collectively expressed by Israel and Christianity in its Lebanese mountain citadel. Africa and Europe, as well as southwest Asia, are linked by history and geography to the destiny of the Middle East.

The states of our region do not have the same points of emphasis in their international relations. Iraq's proximity to Turkey and Iran, Egypt's problems in relation to Sudan, Ethiopia and Libya and the preoccupations of Tunisia and Morocco with French attitudes and policies are all of particular concern to the States concerned, and of more academic and detached interests to States further afield.

XI

The national movement leading to Israel's rebirth arose simultaneously with the renaissance of Arab nationalism. An affirmative attitude to Arab nationalism can be expected from Israel, provided that we speak of the rights of each Arab nation to live in sovereignty and peace. But there is room for criticism of two tendencies in Arab nationalism today.

The first is a lack of altruism. This nationalism does not recognize for others the rights which it asserts for itself. There are many who follow Arab nationalism into the meaningless assertion that Israel is the "cause" of the ferment and rancor which mark Arab nationalism today. There are even some who say that the problems of the Middle East are largely a result of

"Israel's existence." It is not clear what deduction could be drawn from this, even if it were true. It could be proved, I suppose, that the Franco-Prussian War was due to the existence of Prussia, if you were a Frenchman, or to the existence of France, if you were a Prussian. Similarly the Cold War today could be described as being due to the existence of the Soviet Union or of the United States. There is little value in a diagnosis which merely defines the "existence" of the contestants as the cause of the contest. In point of fact no international problem has ever been caused by Israel's existence. Many international problems have been caused by a refusal to recognize that existence, and to establish with Israel the peaceful relations dictated by the United Nations Charter. It is morally and legally inadmissible to take the "existence" of ten Arab states for granted and to regard Israel's statehood as controversial or historically optional. Arab nationalism violates its splendid chance of universal sympathy when it disputes the sovereign equality of all established states.

A second weakness in Arab nationalism is its failure to understand the social and economic factor in the responsibility of national leadership. Throughout Asia and Africa nationalism is envisaged in purely institutional terms. Liberation is believed to be a function of political freedom alone. Deep exhilaration attends all the emblems of newly won national freedom—the new stamps, coins, flags, parliaments and constitutions. But behind this façade of institutional liberation the old squalor, the old poverty, the old exploitation, the old illiteracy endure—sometimes even aggravated by the transition from colonial rule to independence. Multitudes in the new liberated continents have awakened to find that a man can be free in every institutional sense, and yet lose the essence of his freedom in the throes of hunger and want. Freedom will only survive in those places where political liberty goes hand in hand with a vision of society, economy and culture, geared to a horizon of expanding progress. It is because its political liberty has revolved in a social and economic void that Asian and African nationalism has been gripped by disillusion, and unable to sustain democratic institutions.

The chief gift that Israel can contribute to the Asian and African States, who are now cementing their relations with her, is an understanding of the social, economic and cultural content of nationalism. For in our concept of nationalism the State was never an end in itself. It was always envisaged as a window looking out on a new vision of society and culture. Newly established nations in Asia and Africa are looking to Israel's experience as a guide to their own quest for a social, cultural and economic content with which to fill the institutional framework of their sovereignty. The Arab world too is alive with a new social ferment. But the policies of its leaders and especially of Nasser are hostile to any emphasis on domestic preoccupations. After a brief and startled glance at his nation's economic problems Nasser fled from the progressive slogans of his own revolution and began to feed his people on a diet of diplomatic shocks and sensations.

Our support of Tunis, Morocco, Libya and Sudan in their quest for membership in the United Nations, and other gestures of tolerance that we have made, find their vindication not in the immediate sequel, but in the long perspectives of a history in which Israel and the Arab world must find a way to each other's comprehension and ultimate trust.

XII

Nasserism with its social apathy, its appeal to demagogy and its ambition for continental domination is not likely to be the agent of an Arab reconciliation with Israel. The trouble is that Arab nationalism has never sought to educate itself in the history of Israel's national origins; has never faced, even as an unpleasant fact, the actuality of our tenacious covenant with our land. Even if they were to study us in an initially hostile spirit, it would be better than for them to refuse to look at us at all, in the hopeless dream that if they pretend hard enough we might fade away. For any serious contemplation of Arab and Israeli nationalism must in the final resort vindicate their compatibility.

I believe that the spectacle of Israel's manifest permanence and stability is beginning to make an impact on thoughtful Arab minds. Peace will be gained not by a direct route which leaps straight towards it, but through the indirect approach of Israel's consolidation. A wave first of reluctant acceptance, and then of understanding, will arise on the outside circle of our region and draw gradually inwards. The non-Arab States of the Middle East, and even the African Arab-speaking States, have never been emotionally identified with the anti-Israel obsession of Cairo, Damascus and Amman. It may take time before an initial passivity flowers into a more affirmative approach. Let us be patient about Arab-Israel relations—and constructively impatient in all the other aspects of our consolidation.

In the mid-Summer months of 1958 the tide of nationalism seemed about to engulf our region and the world in violence. Now the peril appears to have subsided. But we have, at best, a brooding tranquility. The three circles of tension in Arab nationalism have not been healed. But we cannot ignore two brighter trends which hold the promise of a better dawn. First, there is a growing tendency of Middle Eastern nations to assert their independence against expansionist forces bent on hegemony and domination. It is sufficient to read reports from Beirut, Amman, Tunis and Khartoum, as well as from the non-Arab capitals of our region, in order to perceive the broadening scale of this resistance to Nasserist hegemony. It seems that Middle Eastern nations with the Syrian precedent before them are not in a mood willingly to renounce their independence, especially after Israel's successful resistance to Nasserism in 1956.

A second element of progress is that the leading Western capitals are now aware that any plan to stabilize the Middle East must include a serious effort to reinforce Israel in all the elements of her strength and spirit. Never has this consciousness been more widespread than today amongst all the leading members of the Western community. The United States, Britain and France are each contributing to Israel's growing strength. It is our ardent hope that this policy will become universal amongst all the members of the United Nations family. A strong demonstration of international support for Israel's independence, integrity and economic progress is more likely than anything else to expedite the inevitable dawn of a peaceful era in the relations between Israel and the Arab world.

XIII

While Israeli nationalism faces some problems similar to those of its neighbors, it has its unique attributes. For centuries Israel's national identity lacked the normal receptacles of territory and political freedom. The nation was carried in the mind and in the heart. Thus Israel's nationalism was marked from birth by an intense spirituality, by a unique capacity to live in a world of ideas remote from concrete forms. The survival of Israel was always regarded not as an ultimate value but as a means to perpetuate certain values and ideals. Such a nationalism would lose its most authentic qualities if it came to regard the fulfilment of statehood as the end rather than as the beginning of its journey. We cannot escape a particular vocation arising from a special lineage. Israel's nationalism is more than a political movement. It is a faith; a religion; a culture; a civilization; a journey together of people across generations of martyrdom; and the intimate covenant born of that journey and from the wondrous arrival at the destination.

In the development of our national life and culture we cannot ignore a background so rich and distinctive. The beginning of the second decade is a suitable point at which to take stock of what we signify for the world and for ourselves. We have received a tribute of friendship beyond the measure of our material and physical dimensions. Never in modern times has a state of two million people and eight thousand square miles become the recipient of such fascinated scrutiny. This has happened because the world sees Israel as endowed with a dimension beyond the perspectives of its limited territory and its population. The sense of having a historic purpose beyond the measure of her size is by far the most important quality for Israel to take with her into the coming years. The first decade is ended. Ended—but in a sense hauntingly alive, and forever unended. As it sinks down beyond the horizon it leaves behind a twilight streaked with fire which will live on, deep in the mind and heart of our nation, as long as any memory of the past endures. Whatever the people of Israel may hereafter accomplish will take form and color from the experience of that first decade. Those years with their joys and sorrows, with their unendurable pathos and their stark and rugged splendor, have become our national possession until the end of time. A new dimension has been added to the people's memory and the exploration of it will take many generations.

Three hundred years ago the Pilgrim Fathers, celebrating their first years of survival after many ordeals, wrote humble words: "We have made a clearing in the wilderness; and another year will see a broader clearing, a better garnering; we have made a good beginning in a hostile world."

So may the people of Israel pause at this milestone in its journey, and in its own language and tradition offer benediction to the providence of its history—which has kept it in life, and sustained it, and enabled it to reach this day.